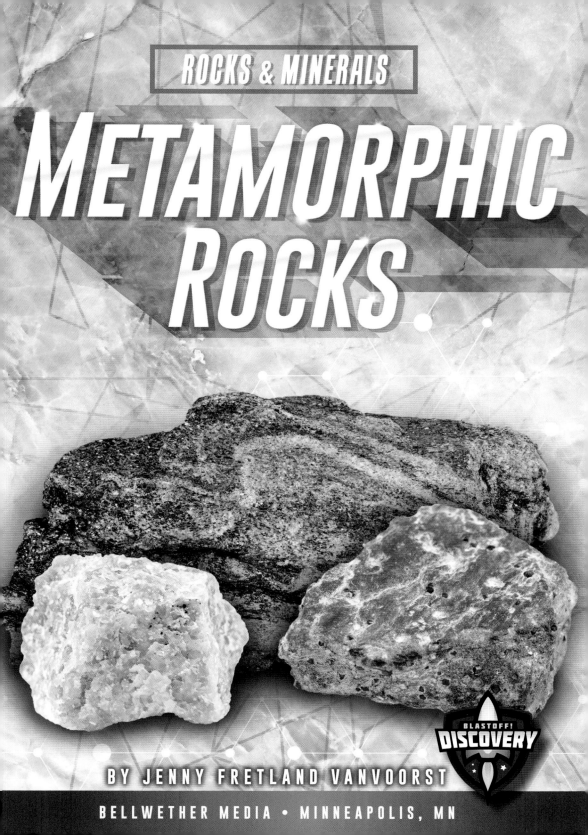

ROCKS & MINERALS

METAMORPHIC ROCKS

BY JENNY FRETLAND VANVOORST

BELLWETHER MEDIA • MINNEAPOLIS, MN

BLASTOFF!
DISCOVERY

Blastoff! Discovery launches
a new mission: reading to learn.
Filled with facts and features, each
book offers you an exciting new
world to explore!

This edition first published in 2020 by Bellwether Media, Inc.

No part of this publication may be reproduced in whole or in part
without written permission of the publisher.
For information regarding permission, write to Bellwether Media, Inc.,
Attention: Permissions Department,
6012 Blue Circle Drive, Minnetonka, MN 55343.

Library of Congress Cataloging-in-Publication Data

Names: Fretland VanVoorst, Jenny, 1972- author.
Title: Metamorphic rocks / by Jenny Fretland VanVoorst.
Description: Minneapolis, MN : Bellwether Media, Inc., 2020. |
Series: Blastoff! Discovery: Rocks & Minerals |
Audience: Ages 7-13. | Audience: Grades 3 to 8. |
    Includes bibliographical references and index. |
    Description based on print version record and CIP
    data provided by publisher; resource not viewed.
Identifiers: LCCN 2019003823 (print) |
    LCCN 2019009556 (ebook) | ISBN 9781618916488 (ebook) |
    ISBN 9781644870761 (hardcover : alk. paper) |
    ISBN 9781618917430 (pbk.)
Subjects: LCSH: Metamorphic rocks–Juvenile literature. |
    Petrology–Juvenile literature. |
    Geochemical cycles–Juvenile literature.
Classification: LCC QE475.A2 (ebook) | LCC QE475.A2 F74 2020
    (print) | DDC 552/.4–dc23
LC record available at https://lccn.loc.gov/2019003823

Editor: Betsy Rathburn   Designer: Jeffrey Kollock

Printed in the United States of America, North Mankato, MN.

TABLE OF CONTENTS

STATUE OF
DAVID IN ITALY

BUILT FROM STONE

LINCOLN MEMORIAL
IN WASHINGTON, D.C.

It is the first day of your trip to Washington, D.C. You have many museum visits planned. You will see art, aircraft, and historic **artifacts**. What a trip!

WASHINGTON MONUMENT

ABRAHAM LINCOLN SCULPTURE

You will also see many **monuments**. The Washington Monument towers above the city. It rises 555 feet (169 meters) high! Nearby, the Lincoln Memorial honors Abraham Lincoln. Behind its tall columns is a large sculpture of the former president. What do these monuments have in common? They are made of marble!

WHAT ARE METAMORPHIC ROCKS?

Metamorphic rocks are one of the three main rock types. They are made up of one or more **minerals**. There are many different metamorphic rocks. Marble, slate, gneiss, and hornfels are some of the most common.

Metamorphic rocks are usually deep below Earth's surface. But these rocks can be found all over the world. Much of Earth's surface is metamorphic rock! These rocks are often found in mountain ranges.

GNEISS FORMATION IN MAINE

METAMORPHIC MIDDLE

Metamorphic rocks make up the core of many mountain ranges. Over millions of years, the mountains erode. The metamorphic rocks come to the surface!

MARBLE CLIFFS IN GREECE

Scientists can identify the different metamorphic rocks. They consider where the rock was found. Some metamorphic rocks are only found in certain parts of the world!

LAPIS LAZULI

Lapis lazuli is a beautiful blue rock often used in jewelry. It is a rare metamorphic rock most commonly found in Afghanistan.

LAPIS LAZULI

They study the rock's features, too. The **Mohs scale** helps scientists rate how hard or soft the rock is. The **texture** tells scientists how large the minerals that make up the rock are. Small minerals mean a fine **grain**. Larger minerals make the rock **coarse**. Other characteristics such as color are also important!

WRITING SLATE

In the 1800s, slate was often used as a writing surface in schools! Students wrote on sheets of slate with chalk.

There are two types of metamorphic rocks. Foliated metamorphic rocks are easy to spot. They have a striped look that comes from different layers of minerals. The stripes may be wavy or straight. They can also be thick or thin. Some stripes are as thin as a sheet of paper!

Some foliated metamorphic rocks break easily along their layers. Slate is a common example. Other foliated metamorphic rocks, such as gneiss, are harder to break!

METAMORPHIC ROCK PROFILE

NAME: SLATE

HARDNESS: around 4 on Mohs scale

1 soft	2	3	4	5	6	7	8	9	10 hard

TYPE: foliated

FOUND: around the world, with major areas in the United States, Brazil, and Spain

MADE OF: quartz, chlorite, calcite, pyrite, hematite, mica, and other minerals

USES: roofing tiles, flooring, electrical work

METAMORPHIC ROCK PROFILE

NAME: **MARBLE**

HARDNESS: 3 to 4 on Mohs scale

1 soft	2	3	4	5	6	7	8	9	10 hard

TYPE: non-foliated

FOUND: around the world, with major areas in Italy, China, Iran, Egypt, and Greece

MADE OF: calcite, quartz, pyrite, and other minerals

USES: flooring, countertops, sculptures

Non-foliated metamorphic rocks do not have visible mineral layers. They are often made up of minerals with large grains. The minerals may be many different colors. But they do not line up in visible bands. Instead, their placement is random.

Non-foliated metamorphic rocks are found around the world. Common examples are marble, quartzite, and novaculite. Each of these rocks can be many different colors!

TAJ MAHAL

AMAZING MARBLE

Many buildings are made of marble. The Taj Mahal in India is one of the most famous marble buildings in the world!

HOW DO METAMORPHIC ROCKS FORM?

FOLIATED SCHIST
CLIFFS IN PORTUGAL

Metamorphic rocks form during a process called **metamorphism**. Heat and pressure change other types of rocks. Igneous and sedimentary rocks become metamorphic rocks!

Metamorphism changes the rocks' structure. In foliated metamorphic rocks, flat minerals are squished into stripes. The stripes fold together and change shape. Non-foliated metamorphic rocks have rounder minerals. Round minerals are harder to squish. These rocks do not form stripes!

NON-FOLIATED QUARTZITE AT PIPESTONE NATIONAL MONUMENT IN MINNESOTA

COOLED LAVA OVER EXISTING ROCKS

There are two kinds of metamorphism. Contact metamorphism usually happens below Earth's surface. It can affect any type of rock. But it often occurs where there is a lot of igneous rock.

Large areas of rock come into contact with **magma**. The magma heats the rock. It becomes metamorphic rock when it cools. Above ground, the same process may happen when a volcano erupts. Lava flows onto existing rocks. The heat changes them into metamorphic rocks!

CONTACT METAMORPHISM

1 HOT MAGMA OR LAVA MELTS EXISTING ROCK

2 MELTED ROCKS COOL INTO METAMORPHIC ROCKS

VOLCANO

COOLING METAMORPHIC ROCKS

MAGMA

Regional metamorphism is also common. Most metamorphic rocks are made in this way. This type of metamorphism happens along **tectonic plates**. These huge pieces of Earth may smash against each other. The **pressure** pushes rocks together. Over time, pressure makes them metamorphic rocks.

REGIONAL METAMORPHISM

1 TECTONIC PLATES SMASH TOGETHER

2 THE HEAT AND PRESSURE CREATE METAMORPHIC ROCKS

OCEANIC PLATE

CONTINENTAL PLATE

METAMORPHIC ROCKS FORMING

TECTONIC PLATE DIVIDE IN ICELAND

!WORLD'S LONGEST

The Andes Mountains make up the world's longest mountain range! It was formed millions of years ago through regional metamorphism.

Other times, one plate may push under another one. The rocks in the lower plate are buried. Pressure and heat build up. The buried rocks become metamorphic!

LIMESTONE TO MARBLE

Heat and pressure turn many
common rocks into metamorphic
rocks. Through metamorphism,
the sedimentary rock limestone
turns into marble!

ERODED LIMESTONE
CAVERN

20

Metamorphism is part of the **rock cycle**. Over time, metamorphic rocks may melt into magma. Magma then cools into igneous rocks. **Erosion** may bring the igneous rocks to Earth's surface.

Even more erosion breaks down igneous rocks. Over millions of years, they break into tiny **sediments**. As the sediments get buried, they crush together into sedimentary rocks. Through millions more years of heat and pressure, the sedimentary rocks may again become metamorphic!

THE ROCK CYCLE

HEAT AND PRESSURE

SEDIMENTARY ROCK

PRESSURE

METAMORPHIC ROCK

EROSION

SEDIMENTS

MELTING

HEAT AND PRESSURE

EROSION

MAGMA

MELTING

IGNEOUS ROCK

COOLING

HOW ARE METAMORPHIC ROCKS USED?

Humans have used metamorphic rocks for centuries. Some Native Americans use quartzite to make **ceremonial** pipes. They create cutting tools from hornfels. Soapstone is used to make bowls and cooking pots!

Other metamorphic rocks have been used, too. Lapis lazuli has been carved into jewelry for hundreds of years. In the year 432 BCE, the ancient Greeks completed the beautiful marble Parthenon!

SOAPSTONE POTTERY

PARTHENON IN ATHENS, GREECE

Today, metamorphic rocks continue to shape our world. Blocks of marble are carved into sculptures and tombstones. Thick marble slabs form countertops. Thin marble tiles cover bathroom floors. Finely ground marble is even used in toothpaste!

MARBLE COUNTERTOP

MARBLE CARVING

Metamorphic rocks are still used in building, too. Slate tiles are a strong material often used in roofing. Quartzite makes a great bed for railroad tracks. Schist is a common landscaping rock!

SLATE ROOF TILES

SCIENTIST WORKING WITH MARBLE

Metamorphic rocks help us understand our world, too. Scientists study the rocks to learn about Earth's natural processes. They learn how mountain ranges form. They also learn about the conditions below Earth's surface.

Scientists also use metamorphic rocks to learn about Earth's past. If metamorphic rocks are found in flat areas, that means a large mountain may once have stood there!

METAMORPHIC ROCK CHOCOLATE FUDGE

MATERIALS

- 1 LARGE GLASS, MICROWAVE-SAFE BOWL
- 1 SMALLER BOWL THAT WILL FIT INSIDE THE LARGE BOWL
- 1 SMALL GLASS BAKING DISH
- PARCHMENT PAPER
- 1 CUP WHITE CHOCOLATE CHIPS
- 1 CUP MILK CHOCOLATE CHIPS
- 1 CAN SWEETENED CONDENSED MILK
- 1 CUP DRIED FRUIT, NUTS, OR CANDY PIECES
- 1 TABLESPOON UNSALTED BUTTER
- 1 TEASPOON VANILLA EXTRACT

METAMORPHIC FUDGE

DIRECTIONS

1. In the large bowl, combine the ingredients. Stir together. These represent sediments.

2. Place a piece of parchment paper over the top of the bowl.

3. Place the smaller bowl on top of the parchment paper. Press down so that the mixture begins to form to the inside of the larger bowl.

4. Microwave the bowls for 1 minute, or until the mixture begins to melt. Remove smaller bowl and parchment paper.

5. Stir the mixture, then press the parchment paper and smaller bowl back down onto the chocolate. This represents the heat and pressure that create metamorphic rocks.

6. Continue heating and pressing until the chocolate is melted.

7. Pour the mixture into the baking dish and cool in the refrigerator. When the mixture is firm, cut into cubes and eat!

ROCK CLIMBER ON GNEISS

MARBLE STAIRCASE

Scientists are still finding ways to use metamorphic rocks. Gneiss is often used during road construction. New technology makes it easier than ever to sharpen quartzite. This rock can be used for precise cutting.

Metamorphic rocks are still used in artwork, too.
Sculptors still use marble to carve beautiful works.
In the future, even more metamorphic rocks will be
used in art, buildings, and beyond!

GLOSSARY

artifacts—objects that preserve the history and culture of a past event or place

ceremonial—related to or used in ceremonies or traditional events

coarse—rough

erosion—the process through which rocks are worn away by wind, water, or ice

grain—the texture or roughness of a rock; the size of a rock's crystals determine its grain.

magma—melted rock beneath Earth's surface

metamorphism—a process of adding heat and pressure during which igneous or sedimentary rocks become metamorphic rocks

minerals—materials that occur naturally on Earth; minerals make up rocks, sands, and soils.

Mohs scale—a scale that measures the hardness of rocks

monuments—buildings or other structures built to honor people

pressure—force

rock cycle—the process through which igneous, sedimentary, and metamorphic rocks change into one another

sediments—tiny pieces of rocks

tectonic plates—parts of Earth that move against and away from one another

texture—a measure of the materials that make up a rock and how they are arranged; texture uses grain size, shape, and arrangement to determine whether rocks are coarse or fine.

LAPIS LAZULI

TO LEARN MORE

AT THE LIBRARY

Nagle, Frances. *What Is the Rock Cycle?* New York, N.Y.: Gareth Stevens, 2018.

Pettiford, Rebecca. *Metamorphic Rocks.* Minneapolis: Jump!, Inc., 2019.

Sawyer, Ava. *Metamorphic Rocks.* North Mankato, Minn.: Capstone Press, 2019.

ON THE WEB

FACTSURFER

Factsurfer.com gives you a safe, fun way to find more information.

1. Go to www.factsurfer.com.

2. Enter "metamorphic rocks" into the search box and click Q.

3. Select your book cover to see a list of related web sites.

INDEX

The images in this book are reproduced through the courtesy of: Tyler Boyes, front cover (left, right); Breck P. Kent, front cover (middle); Gilmanshin, p. 3; S.Borisov, pp. 4, 5; Arianna Tonarelli, p. 5 (Lincoln Memorial); dibrova, p. 5 (Washington Monument); Colin D. Young, p. 6; Porojnicu Stelian, pp. 6, 7; Jiri Vaclavek, p. 8; AlbertoLoyo, p. 9; Senata, p. 10 (frame); Gerry Bishop, p. 19; boonchai sakunchonruedee, p. 11; Mrs_ya, p. 12; Tanarch, p. 13; Juan Vilata, pp. 14, 15; PBouman, p. 15; George Burba, p. 16; Benedikt Juerges, p. 19; Natasa Kirin, p. 20 (frame); Jarun Tedjaem, pp. 20, 21; Fokin Oleg, p. 21 (sedimentary); milart, p. 21 (metamorphic); bigjom jom, p. 21 (magma); Vladislav S, p. 21 (igneous); bogdan ionescu, p. 21 (sediments); Horus2017, p. 22; Samot, pp. 21, 22; Yolanta, pp. 24, 25; Nongnuch_L, p. 24 (counter); PointImages, p. 24 (carving); MediaWorldImages/ alamy, p. 26; Nagel Photography, p. 28 (staircase); LOOK Die Bildagentur der Fotografen GmbH/ alamy, p. 28 (rock climber); marekusz, pp. 28, 29; Bjoern Wylezich, pp. 30, 31.